BUT YOU DID NOT COME BACK

BUT YOU DID NOT COME BACK

MARCELINE LORIDAN-IVENS

WITH JUDITH PERRIGNON

TRANSLATED FROM THE FRENCH BY
SANDRA SMITH

Atlantic Monthly Press
New York

First published in French as *Et tu n'es pas revenu* by Éditions Grasset & Fasquelle

Printed in the United States of America

ISBN 978-0-8021-2450-0
eISBN 978-0-8021-9065-9

Atlantic Monthly Press
an imprint of Grove Atlantic
154 West 14th Street
New York, NY 10011

Distributed by Publishers Group West

groveatlantic.com

16 17 18 19 20   10 9 8 7 6 5 4 3 2 1

BUT YOU
DID NOT
COME
BACK

I was quite a cheerful person, you know, in spite of what happened to us. We were happy in our own way, as a revenge against sadness, so we could still laugh. People liked that about me. But I'm changing. It isn't bitterness, I'm not bitter. It's just as if I were already gone. I listen to the radio, to the news, so I'm often afraid because I know what's happening. I don't belong here anymore. Perhaps it's an acceptance of death, or a lack of will. I'm slowing down.

And so I think about you. I can picture the note you managed to get to me back there, a stained little scrap of paper, almost rectangular, torn on one end. I can see your writing, slanted to the right, and four or five sentences that I can no longer remember. I'm sure of one line, the first: "My darling little girl," and the last line too, your signature: "Shloïme." But what came in between, I don't know anymore. I try to remember and I can't. I try, but it's like a deep hole and I don't want to fall in. So I concentrate on other things: Where did you get that paper and pencil? What did you promise the man who brought me your message? That may seem unimportant today, but then, that piece of paper, folded in four, your writing, the steps of the man walking from you to me, proved that we still existed. Why don't I remember? All I have left is Shloïme and his darling little girl. They were deported together. You to Auschwitz, me to Birkenau.

Afterwards, history linked those two places with a simple hyphen. Auschwitz-Birkenau. Some people just say Auschwitz, the largest death camp of the Third Reich. Time obliterates what separated us, it distorts everything. Auschwitz was built behind a little town; Birkenau was in the countryside. It was only when you went out through the large gate with your work detail that you could catch a glimpse of the other camp. The men from Auschwitz looked toward us and thought: That's where our wives, our sisters, our daughters died; and that's where we'll end up, in the gas chambers. And I, I looked toward you and wondered, Is it a camp or a town? Has he gone to the gas chamber? Is he still alive? Between us stood fields, prison blocks, watchtowers, barbed wire, crematoriums, and above all else, the unbearable uncertainty of what was happening to us all. It was as if we were separated by thousands of kilometers. The books say it was barely three.

There were very few prisoners who could move between the two camps. He was an electrician; he changed the odd lightbulb in our dark prison block. He appeared one evening. Or it might have been a Sunday afternoon. Anyway, I was there when he came, I heard my name, Rozenberg! He came in, he asked for Marceline. That's me, I replied. He handed me the scrap of paper, saying: "This is a message from your father."

We only had a few seconds, we could have been killed for that simple act. And I had nothing to answer you with, no paper, no pencil, objects no longer existed in our lives—they formed mountains in the storehouses where we worked, objects belonged to the dead. We were slaves: all we had was a spoon wedged into a seam, a pocket, or a shoulder strap, and a band tied around our waist— a bit of fabric torn from our clothes or a thin rope found on the ground—to hang our metal bowl from. So I took out the gold coin I'd stolen while I was sorting out the clothes. I'd found it in a hem, hidden as if it were some poor man's treasure, and I'd wrapped it up in a piece of cloth; I didn't know what to do with it, or where to hide it, or how to trade it on the camp's black market. I handed it to the electrician, I wanted him to give it to you, I knew he'd steal it, everyone stole in the camp; in our block, you could always hear people crying: "Someone stole my bread!" So I stammered in a mixture of Yiddish and German I'd learned in the camp that if he intended to keep it, he should give you half. Did you get it? I'll never know. I read your note right away, I'm sure of that. I didn't show it to anyone but I told everyone there, "My father wrote to me."

Other words you said haunted me then. Those words were more important than anything. You said them at Drancy, when we still didn't know where we were going. Like everyone else, we said over and over again: "We're going to *Pitchipoï*," that Yiddish word that stands for an unknown destination and sounds so sweet to children. They would use it when they talked about trains as they set off: "They're going to *Pitchipoï*," they'd say out loud, to reassure themselves after the adults had whispered it to them. But I was no longer a child. I was a big girl, as they say. In my bedroom at the château, I'd redecorated, put a stop to my dreams, got rid of my toys, drawn many Crosses of Lorraine on the wall, and hung pictures above my sky-blue desk, portraits of generals from the first war—Hoche, Foch, Joffre—left in the attic by the previous owner. Do you remember when the principal of the school in Orange asked to see you? She'd found my private diary that was full of dark rumors and reproaches about the chief supervisor and certain teachers, but most importantly, a fierce defense of de Gaulle. "Your daughter will have to appear before the disciplinary committee; it would be better if you withdrew her from school," she'd said, in order to protect us. She gave you my diary. You probably read it and found out I was in love with a boy I met on the bus that took us back to Bollène after school; I gave him my bread ration tickets and in exchange, he did my math homework. He wasn't Jewish. You didn't speak to me for two months after that. We'd reached the age when we would fight, a father and his fifteen-year-old daughter.

So at Drancy, you knew very well that nothing escaped me when I saw you and the other men looking so serious, grouped together in the courtyard, united by a whisper, by the same premonition that the trains were headed far away to the east and the lands you all had fled. "We'll work over there and we'll see each other on Sundays," I'd said. And you'd replied: "You might come back, because you're young, but I will not come back." That prophecy burned into my mind as violently and definitively as the number 78750 tattooed on my left arm a few weeks later.

That prophecy became a terrifying companion, in spite of myself. I clung on to it sometimes; I loved those first words when my friends, and the ones who weren't my friends, disappeared one by one. Then I rejected your prophecy, I hated the words "I will not come back," words that condemned you, separated us, seemed to offer up your life in exchange for mine. I was still alive— were you?

Then there was the day when we passed each other. My work detail had gone to break up stones, pull along small trucks, and dig ditches along the new road for Crematorium number 5, and we walked in rows of five, as always; we were going back to the camp. It was about six o'clock in the evening. Do you know that this moment we shared doesn't belong to just us? That it is part of the memories of the people who survived and is mentioned in their books? For all the dreams of being reunited burst forth in the camp of industrial death, the bodies of all our family who were still alive shuddered when we saw each other, when we broke free from the ranks and ran toward one another. I fell into your arms, fell with all my heart—your prophecy wasn't true, you were alive. They could have judged you useless from the moment you'd arrived, you were in your early forties, a bad hernia in your groin meant you had to wear a belt, there was a long scar on your thumb from when you were injured at the factory. But you were still strong enough to be their slave, like me. You were meant to live, not to die. I was so happy to see you! Our senses came alive again, the sense of touch, the feel of a body we loved. That moment would cost us dearly, but for a few precious seconds, it interrupted the merciless script written for us all. An SS officer hit me, called me a whore, for the women weren't allowed to talk to the men. "She's my daughter!" you cried, still holding me tightly in your arms. Shloïme and his darling little girl. We were both alive. Your logic didn't hold up anymore, age had nothing to do with it—no logic existed in the camp, the only thing that counted was their obsession with numbers. We'd either die right away or a little later, but we wouldn't make it out alive. I had just enough time to give you the name of my prison block: "I'm in 27B."

I was beaten so hard that I fainted, and when I came to, you were gone, but I found a tomato and an onion in my hand that you'd secretly slipped to me—your lunch, I'm sure—and I hid them right away. How was it possible? A tomato and an onion. Those two vegetables hidden beside me made everything possible once more, I was a child and you were my father again, my protector, the one who kept me fed, the head of a business that manufactured sweaters in his factory in Nancy, the slightly crazy man who bought us a little château in the south, in Bollène, and took me there in a horse-drawn carriage, looking all mysterious, so happy about your surprise that you asked: "What do you wish for most in the world, Marceline?"

The next day, our work details passed each other again. But we didn't dare move. I saw you in the distance. You were there, so close to me, very thin, wearing a baggy striped uniform, but still a magician, a man who could astonish me. Where did you get the tomato and onion that brought such joy to my stomach and a friend's? All we were given was some murky, warm liquid when we got up, a little of which I kept to wash myself with, then soup at noon, a piece of bread in the evening, and once a week either a grayish slice of imitation sausage, a teaspoon of beet jam, or a bit of margarine to spread on two slices of bread. Where did you get the paper to write to me? We had nothing to wipe ourselves with in the latrines. I used to tear off little strips of material from a pair of stained men's underpants that was thrown in my face when I arrived, only too glad to use it up a little at a time to wipe my bottom, but I felt embarrassed and ashamed.

I don't know how much time passed between those two moments, those two gestures, the last between us. Several months, I think. Perhaps less. You remembered my block number, the first in the row closest to the crematorium, and you had the message brought to me. You didn't sign it "Papa" but your first name, in Yiddish, "Shloïme," that became Solomon in France. You had returned to the land where you were born, which hadn't waited for the Nazis to persecute the Jews; you surely needed to affirm your identity, your Jewishness, in this universe where we were nothing more than *Stücke:* things. Perhaps you even found some of your relatives again in the camp, cousins from Poland who always called you Shloïme. Still today, whenever I hear the word "Papa," I'm startled, even seventy-five years later, even when it is spoken by someone I don't know. That word disappeared from my life so early that it hurts, and I can only say it deep in my heart, never out loud. And I certainly couldn't write it down then.

In your message, you must have begged me to hold on, to live. Such ordinary words, words used instinctively, the only words reasonable men have left when they can't imagine the future. You must have used the imperative form of those verbs. But I probably didn't believe what you wrote to me. Not as much as I believed in a tomato or an onion. Words had deserted us. We were hungry. The massacre had started. I'd even forgotten Mama's face. So perhaps your message had too much warmth at once, too much love; I drank it in as soon as I'd read it, like a robot that is hungry and thirsty. And then I erased the memory of it. Thinking about it too much meant letting in the loss, it made me vulnerable, brought up past memories, made me weak, brought death. In life, real life, we also forget, let things slide, make distinctions, trust our feelings. But there, it was the opposite. The first things we lost were the feelings of love and sensitivity. You freeze inside so you don't die. There, you know very well how the spirit shrivels, the future lasts for five minutes, you lose who you are.

I never called out for you to help me. And whenever I thought of you, I pictured you with my baby brother; he was four and I couldn't remember his name anymore. Michel. He never left your side for a second before we were arrested; wherever you went, he was in your arms or at your feet, his hand in yours, as if he were afraid of losing you. Perhaps I hid a little bit of myself in his tiny form. That was another way of calling out to you. I was your darling little girl. Even at fifteen. At any age. I had so little time to save enough of you within me.

From my cell block, I could see the children walking to the gas chambers. I remember one little girl clinging to her doll. She looked lost, staring into space. Behind her were probably months of terror and being hunted. They'd just separated her from her parents, soon they'd tear off her clothes. She already looked like her limp, lifeless doll. I watched her. I knew what chaos and anguish runs through a little girl's mind, knew how determined she was, clutching her doll in her hand. Not long before, a few years earlier, I too had left with a suitcase that had a baby doll inside it, and a little box to keep fishing flies in.

You must have told me you were still alive in that letter, and not very far away. And promised that soon the war would be over and we'd be free. When was that letter? Summer of '44? A little later? We knew about the landings and the battles. The news came into the camp with the latest convoys. Every time, one of us would try to slip into Cell Block A,* where the new arrivals were still in quarantine, living on borrowed time, between the gas chamber and hard labor. We'd look for familiar faces. We always came back with information. That was how we found out that Paris had been liberated, that General Leclerc's troops had

---

* The women's cell block (Trans.)

paraded down the Champs-Élysées; and the next day, we'd all very quietly sung the "Marseillaise" as we passed the orchestra that played military marches and pieces of classical music when we left for work every morning and when we returned at night.

But hearing news from a world we didn't belong to anymore wasn't really important. The gas chamber still hung over us, menacing. We were all on the brink. We only lived in the present, minute by minute. Nothing could give us hope anymore. Hope was dead.

The Hungarians had arrived. Hundreds of thousands of them—you remember that flood of people, as if entire cities were pouring into the camp. Everything increased, both the numbers and the pace. They undressed them, sent them to the gas chamber—the children, babies, and old people first, as usual. The ones death would claim a few days later were penned up in a part of the camp that had just been constructed, the first section of a new camp, close to the crematorium. We called it Mexico.* We walked by it every day on the way to work. We were going to Canada, which is what the Polish women had named the place where we sorted through the clothes, because it was the least difficult job, the one we all hoped for, where we might come across an old crust of bread in a pocket, or a gold coin sewn into a hem. The French women among us would have called it Peru. Strange geography in the miniaturized world of the camp, in Polish. I didn't know why, but Mexico implied impending death.

When we passed by, some of the women would come closer to the electrified fence and whisper questions to us; they didn't have their children anymore, but still wanted to hope. We'd ask them if they had a number. No, they'd reply. Then we'd raise our arms to the heavens as a sign of despair. Our tattooed number was our opportunity, our

---

* A reference to section BIII, begun by the SS in 1944 and never completed (Trans.)

victory, and our shame. I'd helped build the second railway line that led directly to the gas chambers where their children had just been thrown. Now I was going to sort through their clothes.

Death regurgitated so many clothes that I'd been assigned to Canada as an extra worker. We sifted through the skirts, underwear, pants, shirts, shoes of everyone who'd been incinerated and whose bodies gave off the smell of burnt flesh, a smell that hovered over the camp, penetrated deep into our nostrils, our bones, our thoughts, day and night, carrying with it the promise of the same fate. We often sorted through tattered clothes, worn-out shoes in suitcases made of cardboard. And they said the Jews were rich!

The worst of the clothes ended up on us, the nicest ones were sent to Germany. We walked around in the rags of our dead, with a red cross on our backs, like you had too. I wore a dead girl's vest, another girl's skirt, the shoes of yet another. But you have to be really alive for objects and clothes to remind you of someone. Back there,

there were too many clothes, they reminded you of no one anymore, the Nazis had turned those clothes into mountains and they rode around them on bicycles, holding a whip, a barking dog in front of them.

And I dreamed of a striped dress like the Aryan women had, that lovely dress was made of a single piece of material, it covered your whole body and had never belonged to anyone outside the camp; I ended up thinking there was something mysterious about that dress—perhaps it was the feeling of belonging that uniforms give you, they tell you where you are and what you are and also that one day you might be able to take them off.

And I stole things. A sweater once. A spoon for a friend. Then the coin, found sewn into a hem, without knowing it would be for you. I remember having no pockets, I didn't know where to put it. I risked a lot if they found it on me. Who could I trust? The majority of the deported women who were put in charge in the blocks were Aryans.

They would have denounced me or taken everything I had. The anti-Semitism in the camp was
terrifying, the Aryans constantly swore at us, the
Polish women, Ukrainians, and the German crim-
inals were the worst of all.

And I knew I couldn't keep the coin for long
because once a month we had to send everything
to be sterilized to avoid getting lice and typhus.
They'd give us dead people's clothes that never fit
me, they were always too big or too long, even the
very first ones I got when I arrived. I'll never forget them: a skirt that went down to the ground, a
small vest, a pair of stained men's underpants that
stank of disinfectant, one flat shoe and another
with a heel, both too big. I still wear a size two; I
haven't grown much since you last saw me.

I think your letter arrived when I was sent to
work on the potatoes. We'd left Canada; some of
the women had been caught stealing and sent to
the gas chamber, the others were punished and
sent to move the potatoes. We walked in single
file, unloading the wagons and carrying the boxes

to the warehouse, using makeshift crates with handles at the front and back. There were Nazis everywhere, to make sure we didn't steal a single potato.

Then there was that day. The little girl. She was holding the front of a crate full of potatoes and I was at the back, she had no strength left, she was shaking and couldn't keep going, the German SS officer behind me hit the back of my neck so I'd move faster, but I didn't want to, the little girl in front couldn't take a single step, I said I could switch places with her, let her take the back, he hit me even harder, called me a dirty Jew, hit me again, so I moved forward and the handle banged into the little girl's back, every blow to my neck forced me to hurt her; she fell down and couldn't get up so the Nazi finished her off with the butt of his rifle. I call her a little girl, but she was no younger and no smaller than me, but so fragile, thinner than me, so I remember her as a child, I think she was Greek, and I killed her.

Then we were sent to the ditches. We had to
dig them with pickaxes. For a long time I told
people they were near the kitchens, for fifty years
I stuck stubbornly to that lie, told it to others and
especially to myself. It was my friend Frida who
made me remember the truth. "They were near
the kitchens," I said. "No, you're making that up,
they were right next to the gas chamber." She was
right. The crematoriums were working nonstop,
they were so overloaded that flames shot out of
the chimneys instead of smoke, and the flames
were too visible, they were a signal to the Allied
planes that were starting to bomb the armament
factories close by. So they changed their method.
The bodies that had been gassed ended up in the
trenches I was digging, sprinkled with gasoline
and reduced to ashes by a sheet of flames, flames
that spread low across the ground and were invis-
ible to the enemy.

After the Hungarians, the ghetto from Lodz
arrived. I saw them walking up to the gas chambers. I thought that relatives I didn't know, my

aunts, uncles, cousins, grandparents, were probably among them. You were from Lodz. I kept working. I struck the ground without looking around me, with no memories, no future, exhausted by not having enough to drink or eat; I dug the ditches where the bodies of fifty distant relatives from Lodz would burn. I lived in the present, in the next heave of my pickaxe or the moment when Mengele, the camp's devil, made us undress and decided who would go to the gas chamber.

No one reacted, not me, not the others, when the *Sonderkommandos** revolted. The Jewish women working in the armament factory had given them gunpowder, but the non-Jewish local Resistance members had refused to give them weapons. The *Sonderkommandos* blew up the crematorium, blew away their shame, for every day, they carried the bodies from the gas

---

* Work details made up of male Jewish prisoners who were forced to help with disposing of the victims of the gas chambers on threat of death (Trans.)

chambers and threw them into the fire. They fled toward the forest by cutting through the barbed-wire fences, they called out to us, begged us to follow them, but we just watched them, exhausted, incapable of following. Anything good no longer seemed to apply to us; it was too late. They were recaptured and killed.

Your letter arrived too late as well. It probably spoke to me of hope and love, but there was no humanity left in me, I'd killed the little girl, I was digging right near the gas chambers, every one of my actions contradicted and buried your words. I served death. I'd been its hauler. Then its pick-axe. Your words slipped away, disappeared, even though I must have read them many times. They spoke of a world that was no longer mine. I had nothing to hold on to anymore. My memory had to shatter, otherwise I wouldn't have been able to go on living.

Mama didn't come for me in Paris. No one was waiting for me. I'd given the phone number of the château, 58, in Bollène, I still remember that, and she finally answered after they'd tried calling her several times with no success. They told her I'd come back and handed me the phone. I immediately asked if you were there. She didn't reply, all she said was: "Come home." I understood by the hesitation in her voice that you hadn't come back, so I told her I didn't want to come home. I don't remember how she reacted. It didn't matter. You were the one I wanted to see. And I would have happily stayed there, at the Lutetia, that luxurious well-established hotel on the Boulevard Raspail that the Germans had made their defense headquarters, and which the Liberation had converted into a center for returning deportees. It was like a space between adjoining rooms. We slept two or three to a room, everyone on the floor, at the foot of the empty beds with their white sheets, unable to bear the feel of a mattress. And all we thought about was eating. Our backs were still there, on the wooden slats of our prison beds, but our stomachs were here; we were torn apart, conflicted. We were miracles.

To everyone in the foyer reading the lists, or on the sidewalks waving signs and photos of their families who'd disappeared, I said over and over again: "Everyone is dead." If they insisted, showing me family photos, I'd calmly say: "Were there any children? Not a single child will come back." I didn't mince my words, I didn't try to spare their feelings, I was used to death. I'd become as hard-hearted as the deportees who saw us arrive at Birkenau without saying a single comforting word. Surviving makes other people's tears unbearable. You might drown in them.

Yet all those people stayed, and every time a new bus arrived full of returning deportees, everyone got excited. At the Lutetia, waiting eagerly still seemed permissible. I had even met the man who was in solitary confinement in the cell next to mine in the Sainte-Anne d'Avignon prison, the first stage of our deportation to the camps. And yet, he'd been condemned to death. I'd never seen his face, we couldn't recognize each other, but in the foyer of the Lutetia, he was looking for me. Everyone was looking for someone, not necessarily a relative, maybe a friend made in a holding camp, or in the hell of a barracks. He was looking for Marceline. I think I told you how I had communicated with him by tapping on the wall of my cell. I used the order of the alphabet since I didn't know Morse code, A was one knock, B was two, and so on. I'd spelled my first name to him that way. Marceline took eighty knocks. It takes a long time, it forms bonds. "They didn't kill me," he said when we found each other, "they deported me to Buchenwald."

And I would have gladly stayed at the Lutetia, let myself get carried along by his story, by the other stories, fleeing my premonition, your prophecy, trying to believe you were still lost in Russia or some other place. Far from life, the life that was asking me to live again, a life full of silences, missing people, deception. The life where you didn't exist.

But the hotel couldn't let me stay. I was given my repatriation papers and put on a train headed south. I didn't want to go—if you only knew how much. The only possible reunion was with you. Sharing things and talking about what had happened was only possible with you. I went back home, a bit of flesh on my body again, they never saw me really thin, my hair had nearly grown back; I was standing in a jam-packed train car, one of the lucky ones, some people said, because I still had a family. But I wasn't really there. I was clinging on to you, which meant I was clinging on to nothing. Eighteen hours later, the train pulled into the station at Bollène. Mama hadn't come to meet me on the platform.

Uncle Charles was there. Later on, he'd tell me what had happened to him, how he'd been at Auschwitz and was then sent to Warsaw to clear away what remained of the ghetto, where the revolt had just been crushed, how he'd run away, hidden in a carriage full of rubble, joined the Polish Resistance, fought with them, all the while hiding the tattooed number on his arm, convinced that they wouldn't want a Jew with them. Right in the middle of the German defeat, he'd taken a boat from Odessa and disembarked with the others at Marseille, but when they explained where they'd come from, they wanted to lock them up in the madhouse. He'd decided it was better not to say a word. That day, when no one was looking, he showed me his tattoo, saying, "I was at Auschwitz. Don't tell them anything about it, they couldn't understand."

Michel was with him. He'd gotten bigger—he was eight. I knelt down in front of him and asked: "Do you recognize me?" He said no, but a few seconds later, he added: "I think you're Marceline."

He looked like a child who'd been abandoned. You were the one he was waiting for.

We set off in silence. Once we'd crossed the bridge over the river Lez, I saw the Château de Gourdon outlined against the hillside. It made me want to turn back. I've never understood that place. I remember the first time you took me there, in a horse-drawn carriage, you were so excited and asked, "What is the thing you wish for most in the world, Marceline?" as if you were about to grant my wish. What did I hope for? The end of the war, that we'd be together, no longer apart, no longer hiding, that was what I wished for and nothing else. But you insisted and spoke in a very mysterious voice: "The place where I'm taking you . . ."

You would have liked to hear me cry out that I'd always dreamed of a house like that. I didn't say it. I wasn't old enough to ask questions, but I didn't understand why you were so excited. We were at war, we were living apart, in hiding, Pétain had come to power, he made us sing

songs at school that I still know by heart, and
you had just bought a château. Did you think that
by becoming the owners of a château we would
no longer be Jews in their eyes? You did know,
though, you read every paper you could. But you
wanted to believe in this country where you'd
settled, you pretended to forget that the château
couldn't legally be yours, for the simple reason
that you were a foreign Jew and didn't have the
right to own property. It was Henri, your eldest
son, who'd signed the title deeds; he'd become a
French citizen when he turned eighteen and had
just been demobilized from a war we'd lost. But
you had proclaimed: "Here, we are free," as if to
justify not having seen things through, to distance yourself as much as possible from the Polish pogroms. You'd planned to go to America but
you'd stopped here, in France, perhaps because
of Zola and his "*J'accuse*," or Balzac, whom you'd
read in Yiddish, you must have told yourself that
nothing could happen to us here. How naïve
you were. Maybe by buying the château and the

vineyards all around it, you were showing some belief in Marshal Pétain, who advocated a return to the land. Or maybe you believed too much in the so-called Free Zone. Or the village's mayor and police chief, who'd promised you they'd give us some warning. We were Jewish and we lived in the most visible of all the houses.

That château was not for you, not for us. And we spent one night too many there. On that night, we'd warned many people not to stay at home, who knows why we decided not to run away until the next day. One more night in this château. One night too many. Did you see how fast they took it away from us? They put everyone they'd just arrested inside, we didn't know them, perhaps they were Resistance fighters or people suspected of helping them; they arrived in groups. You were still groggy from the violent blow to your head from the butt of the rifle and I was clumsily packing our suitcases when a German said, "Take sweaters, it's cold where you're going." They confiscated our house in front of our very eyes, and as Mama and Henriette watched, hidden in the bushes farther away; it was no longer our home, it never had been. Or for barely two years. The Germans set up their headquarters there.

We made our way home almost in silence, me, Michel, and Uncle Charles. Mama was in the courtyard. She took me in her arms. "I can't stay here," I said right away. I added that you wouldn't be coming back. Your prophecy burned in my throat. "Rest for twenty-four hours and then we'll see," she replied. That made no sense. She was playing for time. She didn't know what to say.

She was one of those generous but brusque people, the kind completely lacking in insight, who block out their emotions, transforming them into laughter or anger. You know very well how she used to suddenly get all upset and lash out, how she would shout and pinch us hard. She had always been more caring toward her sons than she ever was toward her daughters, for we were nothing more than an extension of herself. She left it to you to teach us affection and authority. She wasn't hard-hearted. I didn't hold it against her that she hadn't come to the Lutetia or to meet us at the station. She didn't understand where I was coming back from, or didn't want to. She would have had to find words and gestures that were alien to her.

They'd been free for a whole year when I arrived. Mama was often away; she was trying to get back her shop in Épinal, and everything they'd stolen from us, to earn a bit of money. Henri was in Paris about to get married, still thrilled by the months he'd spent with the FFL, the French Resistance, carried along on the postwar wave of amnesia and anti-Semitism that made everyone believe in a heroic France that clashed brutally with every one of my memories. Jacqueline was at boarding school in Orange, Michel was at Henriette's house; I saw them on weekends.

They had the imagination of the very young, saying that one day you would suddenly appear out of the blue, that now you were just sick and lost, far away, very far away, unable to tell anyone your name or address. Michel often wanted

to go to the station and look for you on the platform. Strangely enough, sometimes I joined them,
embraced their illusions, their fantasies, not for
long, just for a few hours, to fall back into childhood again. Sometimes Jacqueline came into my
room, she was thirteen and asked me questions
about what had happened to me, she was the only
one who did; I talked to her but I don't remember
what I said, whether I protected her or not. I'd
also started writing, but always tore everything
up. No one wanted my memories. We didn't have
any memories in common; we should have been
able to add our memories to theirs, but instead,
they pushed us apart.

So I wandered through the château alone during the week. At night, I had horrible nightmares.
I didn't go out during the day, I was afraid to cross
the bridge, to run into the locals. I wandered
through the house panic-stricken, the house that
was too big with its two stories and twenty rooms,
its tower, the enormous vineyards all around it.
Everything came back to me, even Henri's bad

jokes about my frizzy hair—"You have to catch
Marceline and stick her at the end of the broom to
brush away the spiderwebs!"—because afterwards
you told him off and protected me. I wasn't running away from ghosts, quite the contrary, I was
chasing after them, after you. Who else could I
share anything with? I told all of them about your
letter; they would have liked to hear what it said,
but I couldn't recall a single word, so they finally
forgot about it. I was the only one who kept that
miraculous feeling I'd had back then, the note I'd
held in my hands, *My darling little girl*. But here,
nothing had any meaning, not the château, not
my return. Henri and I both seemed destined to
the same sense of loss, the same curse, destined
to dust.

I was too young then to instinctively imagine what that château could tell me about you.
I only understood much later: You'd found an
estate equal in stature to the man you dreamed of
becoming. You have to grow old to truly understand your parents' thoughts. I know that when

you were a young man in Poland, you loved to wear an English top hat and carry a cane, but in secret, because of your strict, austere, very religious father; you'd shaken off the yoke of arranged marriages, married Mama because you loved her. You wanted to be a modern man. Then you'd fallen madly in love with that château, with its tower that would be the symbol of your freedom, your success. It was your dream, not mine, the one you were pursuing the day you took me there for the first time. "What do you wish for most in the world, Marceline?" No one ever asked me that question again.

What I would have liked when I came back was to be treated like an orphan. The orphans went to a sanatorium, they were still together and I often used to think about them. As for my friends, the ones who had died as well as the ones who'd come back, we were a close group, united by suffering; never had I felt as loved as I had back there. I know now that they were my family, more than my family was. "Say I'm your sister,"

Françoise had whispered to me in the camp when a messenger from the SS had asked for my number. She undoubtedly had wanted to do something to help me, or at least, that's what Françoise and I thought; when they ask your number, it's probably a good sign. "Say I'm your sister," she'd whispered.

We'd been friends since Drancy. When we'd arrived at the camp, she forced me to walk when I wanted to get into the truck that would have taken me straight to the gas chamber, and later, when I was very sick and didn't want to go to the infirmary, she'd traded my bread for some aspirin, even though she could have just eaten it herself. But I didn't say she was my sister. I was alone, I was only responsible for myself, my only family then was you. I've always thought it was my fault if they sent her to the gas chamber. Françoise and her beautiful blue eyes haunted me for a long time, like a reprimand, a sister in misfortune.

So I would have been happy to be on a bed in a sanatorium, with the others, talking to them about Françoise and about my selfishness, listening to them tell me that it wasn't my fault, that we were innocent, watching our hair grow back, pouring out memories to women who could bear to hear them and were able to understand. We were coming back to life again, making different choices, the camp hadn't wiped out all of our backgrounds and personalities, but I would have really liked to be in the same place as them, just for a little while, far away from the château, from my mother, from the world that looks down so haughtily at the fate of young women.

Almost immediately, Mama very quietly asked me if I'd been raped. Was I still a virgin? Good enough to be married off? That was her question. That time, I did resent her. She'd understood nothing. Back there, we were no longer women, no longer men. We were the dirty Jewish race: *Stücke*, stinking animals. We stripped naked only when they were deciding when we'd be put to death.

But after the war, the obsession of the Jews to rebuild everything at all costs was intense, extreme—if you only knew. They wanted life to continue normally, as before, they went about it so quickly. They wanted weddings, even though people were missing from their photos because they hadn't come back—weddings, couples, singing, and, soon, children, to fill the void. I was seventeen, no one even thought about sending me back to school and I didn't have the strength to ask. I was a young woman, soon they'd marry me off.

If you had been there, you wouldn't have been able to bear her questions, you would have told Mama to be quiet. You also would have told her to let me sleep on the floor. She didn't want to understand that I couldn't stand the comfort of a bed anymore. "You have to forget," she'd say. Maybe you would have found it difficult to lie in a bed beside her. You would have wanted to sleep on the floor like me, you would have run away from the nightmares that catch up to us and punish us when the sheets are too soft. I even sometimes tell myself that you would have sent me back to school, I missed it so much afterwards; you would

have understood me better than anyone and forgiven me everything. I'm dreaming, no doubt.

But there would have been two of us who
knew. Maybe we wouldn't have talked about it
often, but the stench, what we saw, the foul smells
and the intensity of our emotions would have
washed over us like waves, even in silence, and
we could have divided our memories in two.

The official document arrived at the château on February 12, 1948: *"The Minister of Former Combatants and Victims of the War confirms the death of Szlhama Froim Rozenberg, born on March 7, 1901, in Nowa Slupia, Poland."* The minister could have simply said you were missing, but he decided you were dead. An administrative slip of the pen by a country that declares your death as if it had arranged it.

I still have that document, with the words *"République Française"* and *"Acte de disparition"* at the top of the page, then the sentence that comes next: *"The Minister officially declares that Szlhama Froim Rozenberg is missing and presumed dead in the following circumstances:*

Arrested in March 1944 at Bollène. Interned in Avignon, Marseille, then Drancy. Deported to Auschwitz in the convoy that left Drancy on April 13, 1944. Transferred to Mauthausen and Gross-Rosen."

I read those words and picture our arrest, the Frenchman who was with the Milice hitting you on the head with the butt of his rifle at the back of the garden, where he stopped us from running away. I see our prisons, the uniforms of the Frenchmen who were our guards at Drancy. I recognize our convoy, number 71. Then your prophecy that comes true. Our paths that go in different directions as the war is ending.

In November 1944, you were still in Auschwitz, me in Birkenau, but not for much longer. I'd been prodded by Mengele's baton and had to turn around, like when I'd first arrived—another weeding out. I thought my time was up, my stomach was bleeding internally from my herniated umbilical cord—the one I'd had the operation for, do you remember? It had opened up again,

Mengele couldn't see it, but when he told me to stand in one of the lines, I thought it was the one going to the gas chamber. But I found myself with some of the others in a freight car instead. I was leaving Birkenau. I was going farther away from you.

I didn't even know which direction the train was headed. After two or three days, it finally stopped in the middle of nowhere. It was very cold. We walked another ten kilometers or so through the forest—the sea wasn't far away, we could smell it through the trees—and we finally arrived at Bergen-Belsen. Once we were there, our eyes and noses knew even before we were told: There was no gas chamber.

No gas chamber. No open jaws where they could throw us at any moment. We young women from Birkenau had escaped the largest death camp. No chimney. No crematorium. No stench of burning bodies. That's why I was singing in the tents they'd set up for us in the snow, even though I was shivering. Nothing more than the usual barbarity: hunger, beatings, sickness, the cold. Even the orders were less strict. We still had chores, but the work details were gone, along with roll call for hours on end in the freezing cold. They'd regrouped us, putting all the French women together.

In my unit we'd elected a leader who spoke German, Anne-Lise Stern. She'd grown up in Germany, her father was a student of Freud, her mother a Socialist; they'd fled to France, where Nazism had caught up to them. Anne-Lise behaved in a way that was compliant but protected us at the same time. Humanity seemed to be stirring once more. It wasn't yet hope: We were sure we wouldn't be gassed, but still not certain they wouldn't kill us.

Two months later, in February, we saw the exhausted faces of the people on the death marches arriving from Birkenau. Among them, I recognized my friend Simone, her sister, and their mother, whom I called Madame Jacob; Madame died a few days later of typhus, on the frozen ground of the camp. They had walked so far. They told us how they'd emptied out Auschwitz and Birkenau before the Russians arrived; the ones who could still stand were forced along the roads by rifles prodding them forward.

You were probably among them. But you were walking in a completely different direction than me. You were going south. I was headed north. I rolled around in the snow naked to kill the lice and get warm. There was nothing to eat anymore, starvation and epidemics took over the work of extermination. The worst butchers from Birkenau had also arrived, and they'd reinstituted their filthy methods, counting and recounting us, still obsessed with numbers, with killing Jews even during their defeat; that's what drove them to make you all die on the roads rather than leaving you in the camps where the Allies could have saved you.

I imagine your body among a column of staggering, emaciated men pushed to the limit by the SS. Auschwitz. Mauthausen. Then Gross-Rosen,

according to the death certificate. How far you
traveled! Hundreds of kilometers toward the
south, then suddenly circling back toward the
surrounded Reich, going north again, even farther north than Auschwitz. That means that you
held up, you walked without falling, without giv-
ing them the chance to kill you along the way. You
must have had some strength left when you left
Auschwitz. You really might have survived.

Where were you when I was leaving? All hell
broke loose at Bergen-Belsen. But I was put on
a train again with my group of French women.
We were going to a Junker airplane factory in
Raguhn, near Leipzig. We were leaving to make
machines for a lost war. My path was like a horrific
decrescendo—Birkenau-Bergen-Belsen-Raguhn—
from an extermination camp to a factory concen-
tration camp. It fits with the promise you made
me: "You're young, Marceline, you'll make it." But
where were you? It was February 1945. According to the history books, that's when the Russian
Army liberated the camp at Gross-Rosen. And

according to your official document, that's the last place there was any trace of you. Were you killed and thrown into the communal graves by the desperate Germans?

Maybe not. Mama insisted on believing someone who said he'd seen you at Auschwitz and that you'd left the camp before the death march in January of 1945, that you'd been seen at Dachau and should have stayed there but that you'd started walking again to help a man who couldn't keep going without you and whom the Germans would have killed. According to Mama, you hadn't been selected to keep walking—you sacrificed yourself. I didn't believe it. In the camps, you didn't choose anything, not even the way you died. But Dachau, that was possible; I read that many people from Gross-Rosen were transferred there. It doesn't matter if we didn't have that in writing. It wasn't possible to establish a real inventory anymore, not in the postwar chaos. The French government probably sent out certificates in bulk, writing down likely names,

places, and dates that weren't necessarily veri-
fied. I don't believe a word of the official history
written by France.

But what does it matter today whether you
died in February or April? Why drag out your suffering? I don't know. It's as if I'm still fighting your
prophecy. My life for yours.

I would like to think you didn't die that February. I was no longer wearing dead people's
clothes then. In Raguhn, I was given a striped
dress, like the one I used to dream about in
Birkenau. There was still a red cross on my back,
a yellow star on my chest, but I didn't notice
them anymore: I had the dress I wanted, and
there were even women guards from the countryside who gave us needles and thread so we
could make them fit. They also gave us each a
whole loaf of bread. We ate it all at once, even
though it was our ration for a week.

On the assembly line, I cut out pieces of a
motor from molds. I was very tiny, so they had
me stand on a bench, but the moving assembly

line seemed to want to devour me; it dragged me along one day and injured me, but someone's hands grabbed me and pulled me back, the hands of fate. I would make it out alive. In the factory, the workers were a mixture of Jews and German civilians. I remember the time one of them gestured that he'd left something for me in a drawer. It was a bag full of cooked potato skins.

Did I feel hope again? I did dare to hide when it was time to leave again, to take a train from Leipzig to some unknown destination. The Americans were only eighteen kilometers away now, we knew that. Renée and I hid in a casket in the detention camp—a casket, even though for the first time in a very long time we imagined we might survive! But they counted everyone again at the Leipzig station; two were missing, they came back, looked for us, found us, threw us into a truck. There were fires everywhere, the Allies' bombings never stopped, Germany was being reduced to ashes. And I thought about Mala, who'd told us to hold on and live.

She was our heroine at Birkenau. She was a Belgian Jew, she spoke several languages, and because of that, she had the right to move around freely, and she took advantage of that to help as much as she could. One day, she ran away with her lover, a Polish Resistance fighter who'd been deported, they disguised themselves as SS officers and left in a car. You must have heard this story: Two people were missing when they took roll call. You know how the Nazis became furious if they lost two people, even if we were already fifty or a hundred thousand—how could we know?— behind their barbed wire. You probably stood for hours on end, like us, while they counted and recounted; I wonder if that wasn't the time when they left us kneeling outside on the ground all night long, fighting with all the strength we had left against the temptation to fall down and be killed.

Mala was caught three weeks later at the Czech border, denounced by Polish farmers. Her lover gave himself up; he didn't want her to think he'd talked. He was hanged right away. She was put in a bunker for weeks, in one of those cells you have to crawl into and where you can't even sit down. And then one day, they ordered the Aryan women locked in their barracks and the Jews brought out in the courtyard in front of Lager B.* There were thousands of us in rows of five, me in front, as usual, since I'm so small. The gallows had been set up, the noose was ready, and the camp's SS officers were right in front of it. Mala arrived standing up in a cart pulled along by some prisoners, she was dressed all in black, her hands tied behind her back—the staging was complete. SS Commandant Kramer shouted that none of us would get out alive, we were nothing but vermin, dirty Jews. And while he was shouting, I saw something running down her body—her blood! Someone had obviously given her a blade of some kind, she'd cut the ropes, then slashed her wrists. She was choosing the

---

* Technically, Lager Blb (Trans.)

way she would die. I was fascinated by the blood running down and that they didn't notice while Kramer shouted how all-powerful he was. Suddenly, one of the officers saw. He grabbed her by the arm, but she broke free, then she slapped him across the face and he fell down, and taking advantage of the few seconds she had during the chaos, she started speaking, in French, "Murderers, soon you'll have to pay," then turning to all of us, "Don't be afraid, the end is near! I know, I was free, don't give up, never forget." They rushed her back into the cart, ordered that we all be locked in our cell blocks. *Blocksperre!* Many rumors followed about how they'd finally killed her, that they'd hanged her somewhere else, or even thrown her into the crematorium while she was still alive. We talked about her for a long time. But we didn't believe her promises.

In the truck taking us to Leipzig, I finally believed what she'd said. Once we got to the station, they threw us into a freight car with the people who had typhus, just like they would have thrown us into the gas chamber if we'd still been at Birkenau. That was the beginning of ten very strange days in our locked freight cars. We hardly noticed there weren't many female German guards anymore; all we did was count the dead bodies that were piling up; there were 120 of us, the disease spread like wildfire, the number of dead grew very quickly, we piled their bodies up against the door, I was alive, breathing, right next to them. But you, where were you? With the dead or among the survivors? In the freight car, that was the only demarcation line that counted while the bombings raged above our heads.

One day, as the train crawled along, as the days seemed to drag on forever, I felt a bit of bread in someone's pocket. It took me some time to get it; I'd rummaged through the pockets of the dead in Canada, but their bodies were no longer there. Finally, I stole it from the dead woman and shared it with Renée. Sometimes the train stopped, they opened the doors, and we begged for some of the water they used to cool the train's engine; I looked for some dandelions, the only edible plant I knew.

When we stopped for good, there wasn't a single German left on the train, just us and the driver. We'd arrived at the Theresienstadt ghetto in Czechoslovakia. Its remaining inhabitants opened the doors of the freight cars, saw the dead bodies roll out, then saw us, the starving animals, eyes enormous in our emaciated faces, and they understood what had happened to everyone who'd been taken away, and what was going to happen to them. They rushed to find us something to eat. Just like animals, the young women in the freight cars started fighting each other for the food. I just watched it all, I didn't fight. That doesn't mean I was better than the others. Or maybe I fought too, but I prefer to forget that. I'm no angel.

I came out of a car full of dead bodies. Alive. "You'll come back, Marceline, because you're young," you'd said. But what about you? Were you still breathing that April of 1945? Typhus took Renée. I had scabies and a bleeding stomach. The Russians finally liberated the ghetto. They immediately decreed that we should be put into quarantine because of the typhus. I fled, because another war was starting that you would never know about, one we could already feel coming. The world was being divided into two blocs—soon the East would be under the yoke of the Soviets and the West under American control.

I walked toward Prague with some others, sixty kilometers away. Once we were there, someone dressed the wound on my stomach. I took the road toward the American zone; we kept walking without knowing where we were going, without knowing how many days we'd been walking, without understanding or realizing what we'd lived through, we dragged ourselves along. We knew the Nazis had lost, but it was too late, much too late to rejoice, our suffering had been too great, all we had left was a feeling of horror and loss. Where were you? All I could think about was you. But I didn't try to find you among the others. That's not how we'd be together again.

We ended up in the Pilsen repatriation camp. There, one of the employees said: "We don't repatriate Jews, just prisoners of war." The prisoners stood up for us, refused to leave without us. I'd gotten to Sarre before anyone asked our address; I was given a skirt, underwear, and an official deportee card. And that was the first time I gave the phone number of the château, 58, in Bollène.

You were already dead. I imagine you looked just like all the corpses I saw scattered along the road as I returned. I can picture your arms outspread, your eyes wide open. A body who'd seen death and then watched himself die. A body no one would ever return to us. When your official document arrived, three years later, we were still hoping you'd come back, but without really expecting you to. Michel stopped asking to go to the station. Henri had married Marie. It was a big wedding. I wore a blue dress, like my sisters.

We'd gone to Paris, stayed at the Hôtel Ter-
minus near the Gare de l'Est. You would have
loved their Jewish wedding, you would have
been proud of your eldest son, a hero of the Free
French Forces, walking down the aisle to his new
life with Marie, who'd been arrested with us at
our house but who'd come back alive along with
the rest of her family. The wedding dinner was
held at a fancy restaurant, the Palais d'Orsay.
Everyone around the tables avoided talking about
the camps. But the dressy clothes were nothing
more than armor. *Their* armor. I didn't believe in
Sunday weddings, in some white dresses thrown
over the clothes from Canada; I still carried the
mountains of clothes that we'd sorted through
on my back, and the stench of burnt flesh that
would stay with me forever. I was resisting their
demand that I live.

Mama also remarried. She did it in secret,
without saying anything. She only told us afterwards. I didn't hold it against her. It was the man
she chose and the way she did it that I didn't like.

He'd lost his wife and five children in the camps. He played cards and sponged off Mama. We didn't like him. How could we? It was a time when I had strange dreams, I think. I went into their room, took down the pictures, especially the one of you and the one of our grandparents. I got you out of the room where she no longer slept alone. I realize now that it happened when your official document arrived. 1948. Maybe Mama needed that document to get remarried.

This is what it said: *"By writing a brief letter to the State Prosecutor, the family may request either a statement declaring a person missing, which, after five years, will be replaced by an official Death Certificate, or they may request an official Death Certificate if the missing person is a French citizen and belongs to one of the following categories: mobilized, prisoner of war, refugee, deportee or political prisoner, member of the Free French Forces or the French Resistance Army, conscripted to do hard labor or refused to work in Germany."*

But you weren't French. You'd made many requests before the war to get the citizenship you'd dreamed of. In vain. You loved this country, I'm not sure it was mutual. I remember your voice, your accent, the words you mangled—you spoke French both well and badly. You were a foreign Jew, that was your only official title, according to the state. So we had to wait five more years for you to be officially declared dead. Mama became a French citizen because she was your wife, the widow of a hero. As for me, I was considered a soldier.

Your name is on the monument to the fallen in Bollène. It was inscribed there a very long time after its construction. It was the mayor who suggested it, but he didn't want your name to stand out as different at all; he wanted you to be included among the men who died for France. I told him it was important that it also said you'd been deported to Auschwitz. He said that wasn't necessary. So I told him I preferred you weren't named at all in that case. In the end, he gave in.

That was less than twenty years ago, just before we were about to enter the twenty-first century; even so long after the war, he didn't want any trace of Auschwitz on the village monument. You didn't really die for France. France sent you to your death. You were wrong about her.

As for everything else, you were right. I did come back.

Jacqueline always sends me flowers on May 10, as if it were my birthday. Every year and that moves me very much. We're very close, different but considerate of each another. We're the only two left. May 10 is the date the Russians liberated me from Theresienstadt. I was born that day. I know that Jacqueline sends the flowers for me but also for her father.

My return is synonymous with your absence. To such an extent that I wanted to obliterate it, to disappear like you did. I tried to drown myself in the Seine two years later, the year Henri got married. It happened a little farther along from the Quai Saint-Michel: I'd climbed over the parapet and was about to throw myself in when a man stopped me. Then I got tuberculosis; I was sent to a chic sanatorium in Montana, Switzerland. Mama sometimes came to see me. I couldn't stand her impatience, the way she had of ordering me to get well and to forget. I was such a burden. I tried to kill myself a second time.

Yet in the camp, I did everything I could to stay alive. Never allowed myself to believe that death would mean peace. Never became that girl I'd seen throw herself against the electric fence. She wasn't the only one, it had become a common expression "to go to the fence," to die quickly, electrocuted or riddled with bullets from the machine guns in the watchtower, ending up in the deep pit dug just in front of the barbed wire fences. Never gave up the will to live, never became like the women who let themselves go, choosing to neglect themselves, a gradual detachment from their bodies, a slower death. They began by not saving some of the water from the bottom of their bowl to wash themselves with, they stopped eating, withdrew. They were called Muslims, I don't know why, another word the Polish women used, perhaps because of the blankets they pulled over their heads. Soon they were even more emaciated than us; they couldn't work anymore and were sent to the gas chamber.

I held on. I did. I fought off sickness and the temptation to let myself go under. For the first time in my life, I fasted on Yom Kippur, to feel more Jewish, to remain dignified in the face of the SS. I made up all sorts of strategies to survive. I might have even started to do that in the train. Do you remember? We had just arrived somewhere, we were exhausted, silent, it was dawn, the train slowed down, I climbed up on someone's shoulders, looked out of the small window; I saw a group of women walking in rows of five, they all seemed to be wearing the same dress, they all had red scarves on their heads, so I said: "We're going to have costumes here." I used words from civilization to describe what would happen to us; I preferred that to the absolute silence that had overwhelmed you and the others. I was already resisting. And when the doors opened, I heard the deportees in their striped clothing whisper to me: "Give the children to the old people, say you're eighteen." I had just turned sixteen at Drancy and I was smaller than normal. An SS officer made me open my mouth three times in a row to see my teeth, and I lied about my age.

Why was I incapable of living once I'd returned to the world? It was like a blinding light after months in the darkness, it was too intense, people wanted everything to seem like a fresh start, they wanted to tear my memories from me; they thought they were being rational, in harmony with passing time, the wheel that turns, but they were mad, and not just the Jews—everyone! The war was over, but it was eating all of us up inside.

I would have liked to give you good news, to say that after having lived through the horrors, waiting in vain for you to come back, we recovered. But I can't. You should know that our family did not survive. It fell apart. You had so many wonderful dreams for all of us, but we couldn't live up to them.

After Henri's wedding, we stayed on to live in Paris, on the second floor of 52 Rue Condorcet. Little by little, we abandoned that château you'd fallen in love with. It became a vacation home, even somewhere that felt was a punishment. Mama sent me there every time I wasn't doing well, as if to harden me up in the atmosphere of your authority and your dreams, which were probably hers as well. We sold it in 1958.

You should have come back. I've always thought it would have been better for the family if you had come back instead of me. More than a sister, they needed a husband, a father. Ever since that prophecy you made at Drancy, I've always thought it was your life for mine. And that's what I could see in Michel's eyes on the platform when he came to meet me with Uncle Charles. You were the one he was waiting for. In Birkenau, I'd forgotten his name, I already told you that, but I associated him with you, like a leg or an arm. I could picture him in his dark velvet short trousers, dragging a toy stick with little yellow chicks as wheels that moved as he walked. The two of you strolled across the fields that surrounded the château, he wouldn't let go of you. Your arrest was an amputation for him. He must have asked for you, they probably told him you'd be coming back. But I was the one he saw on the platform. He was still so small, so fragile.

Very soon afterwards, he started showing disturbing signs that we didn't take seriously enough. He didn't manage to stay at boarding school for long, he kept to himself, refused to wash. So Mama brought him home and left him with Henriette. They dealt with his sadness the way they did with my memories. After you were gone, our family became a place where you screamed for help but no one heard, not ever. As a young man, he took refuge for a while in the pseudo-lightheartedness of Saint-Germain-des-Prés, but your absence was eating away at him. His pain festered and worsened. He started toying with the idea of suicide. He ended up becoming a manic-depressive. I tried to take care of him, but when he was having a crisis, I was the one he targeted: He drew swastikas on my letter box or left messages on my answering machine, imitating the voice of an SS officer and barking, "You will be on Convoy 71 with Madame Simone Veil." He even had "SS" tattooed on his arm. He played at being the executioner to be closer to the victim, closer to you. He held it against me that I went with you, that I'd taken his place, the child who follows in your footsteps. In any case, that's how I understood it. He was sick from the camps without ever having been there. When he got to be the age you were when you disappeared, he took some pills and alcohol, this time enough so he wouldn't wake up again. We only broke down his door and found his body inside a full month later. We buried him in the Jewish cemetery in Pantin. He'd always said, "I'll die at the same age as my father."

Mama died two years after him. Then Henriette, a few weeks later. She committed suicide when she was sixty. The same cocktail as Michel. She also died from the camps without ever having been there. Died because she couldn't talk to you, explain anything to you, be with you again. You never should have thrown her out the way you did at the beginning of the war because she'd fallen in love with that soldier who was her pen friend; he wasn't Jewish, she was afraid you'd be angry, so she'd married him in secret. You were furious, threw her out. You shouldn't have done that, just as you shouldn't have taken her out of school when Michel was born so she could take care of him. She was so brilliant. I'm writing to you from a time when women have earned their place in the world; I would have liked you to experience it, to be moved by it, so you could hear and understand the dreams of your daughters: Henriette, Jacqueline, and me. Henriette had great courage. She'd joined the Resistance. When I came back, I found out that when we were arrested, she'd managed to learn that we'd be transferred to Marseille by bus before being sent to Drancy. So she'd tried to mobilize her network to rescue us, she wanted to attack the bus, free us, and come back home to live with us. She left her soldier after the war, left him in order to be forgiven, to reclaim her place in the family, but there was no place to reclaim. Because there was no family without you.

If we'd had a grave, somewhere we could cry over you, perhaps things would have been easier. If you had come home, weak, sick, to die like so many others—for coming home didn't mean surviving—we could have watched you leave us, we could have held your hands tightly until there was no strength left in them, watched over you day and night, listened to your last thoughts, heard your final goodbyes, the words you whispered, that would have made me forget, once and for all, the letter I miss so much today; it would have appeased Michel, reassured Henriette, given all of us the same single image of your death. And we would have closed your eyes while saying Kaddish. As children, we knew about death and its rites: the black flag, the hearse that moves slowly down the street. We would encounter death and respect it, we were much stronger than people are today, they're so afraid of death—if you only knew how much. But it wasn't death that took you away. It was a great black pit and its smoke, and I had looked down into its very depths. It hadn't yet finished its evil task: Even when the war was over, it still seemed to be sucking us in.

Michel and Henriette died because you disappeared. They always missed the last words you never said, words they would have remembered all their lives, words that would have explained their place in this story and in the world. I have a story. I do. I'm the survivor. I know where you died and why. Most importantly, I have pieces of you that belong only to me. Your last steps, your last words, even if I've forgotten them, your final gestures, your last kisses.

We'd both run to the back of the garden that night, and the French policeman caught us behind the gate. We were transferred together to the Sainte-Anne prison in Avignon. There, you'd kissed me, you said we'd try to escape, you wrote letters to Mama, one of which got sent thanks to an Austrian soldier in the Wehrmacht; he'd cried when he saw us arrive—I reminded him of his little redheaded girl. "You won't be coming back from where you're going," he'd said to you, "you have to escape before you get there." We were able to see each other once in the outhouses, I knew where your cell was, so when I was sent to mop the floors in the hallways, I'd sing "*O sole mio*" really loud, so you'd hear me coming, and one of my girl scout songs too, "We can only see the sky, only feel the sun, Goodbye, goodbye, We're off to find the wind, the mountain road is long." Why can I still remember that stupid propaganda song but none of your final words to me?

I don't think I ever told you what I scratched on the wall of my cell in Sainte-Anne. *It's almost a joy to know how unhappy a person can be.* I don't know what the prisoners who took my place after-wards thought, the ones there during the war, or in peacetime, whether they agreed or not, if they understood what it meant. For the happiness I was thinking of was the joy of being with you. I didn't yet know where I was going, the bus that would transfer us to Marseille, the third-class carriage on the train to Drancy, then Convoy 71, at least fifteen hundred people deported to Auschwitz-Birkenau, you and me and about sixty others in a cattle car with all those useless suitcases, and at the end of the first day, I was the one who cried out that I was thirsty. A man slapped me across the face, "Everyone here is thirsty, so shut up!" and you didn't react, you were right, I was learning, we were heading for hell and I had to get used to it. But I said what I'd written again, after the war, in spite of the consequences, in spite of my fear of the gas chamber, the crematorium, the indelible scars on my body and in my mind, I said it again, even more clearly: I loved you so much that I was happy to be deported with you. And I can say it again now. For with time, the darkness of the camps over my life has merged with your absence. And it is having to live without you that weighs down on me.

Your picture is in my room now. I inherited it after Mama died. It's a photo taken in the 1930s: All you see is your chest and head; the picture doesn't show that you were of average height. You're wearing a dark pin-striped suit, you look strong. I put it above my dresser. On the opposite wall, I hung a drawing of a naked woman—she's lying stretched out, smiling, languorous; I left it to her to entice you. So that you'd stop looking at me. So I could get undressed in peace without you seeing me.

I don't like my body. It's as if it still bears the mark of the first man who ever looked at me, a Nazi. I'd never been seen naked before that, never, especially not with my new young woman's body that had just given me breasts and all the rest; modesty was obligatory in the family. So for a long time, I associated getting undressed with death, with hatred, with the icy stare of Mengele, the camp demon who was in charge of the selection, who made us turn all around, naked, prodded by his baton so he could decide who would live and who would die. I think he inspected me when I first arrived and again when I left the camp. The others said, "That's Mengele," I didn't know what he looked like, but after the war I recognized him: his black hair with not a single strand out of place, his cap tilted slightly to one side, his eyes that looked right through you, then sent you to the right or to the left, without you knowing which of the lines would lead to death. I used to pinch my cheeks to give them some color before standing in front of him and his team of SS doctors as they sized us up, scornful and mocking; I tried to hide my wounds, my infected, festering boils, I wanted to show him a body that was still beautiful, still strong.

My frozen toes will be numb forever. The infections left whitish circles on my arms and legs where the skin is fine and limp. For a long time, I had marks on my neck where I'd been hit with batons. And if I've remained hard, thin, it's because I've often stood in front of my mirror, ten, twenty, or thirty years later, and thought, Have to stay slim and svelte so I don't get sent to the gas chamber next time.

I never had children. I never wanted any. You would have reproached me for that, of course. The body of a woman—mine, my mother's, the body of all the others whose stomachs swell up and then empty—was distorted by the camps, forever. I find flesh and its elasticity horrifying. Back there, I saw skin, breasts, and stomachs sag, I saw women hunched over, crumpled up, I saw bodies deteriorate so quickly, become emaciated, disgusting, the road to the crematorium. I hated being herded together, the intimacy that was violated, the deformity, the light touch of bodies nearing the end. We were mirrors for each other. The bodies around us were a forewarning and brought us closer to what we were becoming ourselves. Not a single woman got her period anymore; some of them wondered if they were putting bromide in our food, but it was just that the natural cycles of life had stopped. Motherhood had no meaning anymore: Babies were the first to be sent to the gas chamber. Once in a while, beauty remained intact somehow, leaving some bodies more dignified than others. "You're too beautiful to die," Stenia had said to my friend Simone. She was a Polish criminal who'd become second in command of the camp. There came a time, though, when you couldn't tell us apart, except to distinguish between those who were holding up and those who'd given in. I was holding up. But I had nothing good to pass on to a child. I've even found it difficult to warm to the children of my brother, my sister, and my friends.

It took many experiences with other people to get used to living, get used to myself. And a lot of time to be able to love. I got involved in other eras, other lives, love affairs that you don't tell your father about, in struggles and revolutions intended to wipe away the past.

Little by little, I allowed myself to be carried along by my generation, its chaos, and I felt what it was like to be young. I wanted to make something of myself, without really knowing what, I wanted to become part of a story that was greater than my own, discover the world, learn, laugh a little, join in the endless discussions in the bistros of Saint-Germain-des-Prés. From the Rue Condorcet where we lived, I'd take the 85 bus to the Latin Quarter, full of students and intellectuals, but also dropouts like me. I could feel the desire to live stirring within me, the desire that made me sing while we were shivering in the snow at Bergen-Belsen.

I tried to push Birkenau into the past, I never talked about it anymore, I hid my number. I was often with a friend, Dora, who had also been deported and come back; she'd lost her mother and her little sister there, she was unhappy, I could sense it. I knew that unhappiness was deeply rooted within us, whatever happened. So, to distance myself from unhappiness, I became the opposite of Dora. She was frightened at the idea of going into cafés, I pushed the doors open proudly in a way that was unusual for girls in those days. I can picture both of us sitting in the

Dupont-Latin. She tried not to draw attention to herself, I sat up tall. Boys came to talk to us, they were carefree, funny, I could have dived into their laughing, joking mouths, I thirsted for lightheartedness and knowledge, two words that summed up Saint-Germain-des-Prés. There we found everything the war hadn't taken with it; anti-Semitism was still strong, but what was important was to talk about things. It was a strange mixture: the bourgeoisie, left-wingers, former Resistance fighters. All around me were a circle of orphans I felt close to, and at the same time, I was fed up with the Jews, fed up with being crowded in, a legacy from the camps. I needed to be with other people.

I especially didn't think about what you would have wanted for me—I feared the answer too much. The same as Mama probably, a nice Jewish marriage and a lot of children. She used to shout and rip up the pants I wore like all the other liberated young women, and she'd tell me off whenever someone came to the house. Marriage wasn't for me. I was headed for a life that you probably wouldn't have approved of. And yet, I like to think that you wouldn't have complained about me. That after what we'd lived through, you would have wanted me to be free. But deep down, I don't know what kind of man you would have been. I feel as if I didn't really know you. We were separated at the very moment when we would have begun to find out about each other. I remember that walk in the woods, the war had already started, you were warning me about boys. I was already pretty shy with other people, and you were very strict. We would have had fights, in any case. I even miss the ones that would have been fierce battles. I would have liked to have doors slammed, to have reconciliations. And then I miss the words we would have spoken as time went on, so we could return to the past and heal its wounds. If I still wonder where I could have lost your letter, if it changes according to the day—Did I hide it under a seat in the steam room when we had to change our clothes? Did I lose it at Bergen-Belsen? In

Theresienstadt?—if I still search deep within my memory for those missing lines even though I'm sure I'll never find them again, it's because they are etched somewhere in the recesses of my mind, the place where I sometimes slip away with the things I cannot bear to share, a blank page where I can still talk to you. I know all the love those lines contained. I've spent my entire life trying to find that love.

I no longer bear your name, and I miss that. But I often add, "*née* Rozenberg"—it means "mountain rose" or "a mountain of roses," it's very beautiful. I bear the names of the men I married. Neither was Jewish, but don't hold that against me. The first was Francis Loridan, I met him when I fell off my bike on the way to the château. He helped me get up, and we got married very quickly. He was an engineer, dreamed of going abroad, hoping I would go with him, but I had no desire to live in the colonies where jobs were created by all the construction going on, no desire to be the wife of one of the white masters, and no desire to leave Paris either. He left for Madagascar while I tried to heal in the cultural and political boiling pot of Saint-Germain; I had one little job after another until the day I found work in television. I never joined him out there, but we didn't get divorced for a long time after our separation, and I kept "Loridan" because it had become my professional name. I must admit that it was useful to me. Anti-Semitism was still very widespread after the war, it was easier to be called "Loridan" than "Rozenberg." My second husband was Joris Ivens. And I must tell you about him.

Joris was thirty years older than me. He'd wandered in from Holland, a poet, an artist, a sturdily built man with long white hair—they called him the "Flying Dutchman." He was born at the turn of the century, like you. During his lifetime, he'd seen the birth of the cinema, he was one of its pioneers, one of the greatest documentary makers, known throughout the world. He'd traveled around the entire planet, told the story of the Spanish Civil War, the struggle of the workers and the liberation of many different peoples. He was a man who was haunted by human poverty; he carried it within him and it constantly tore him apart. Like many artists between the two wars, he became a great supporter of the Communist Party, in reaction to the rise of various forms of fascism. He suffered when he saw the party's ideals destroyed by the Soviet system, but he remained a member. I met him in 1962. He'd seen me in a movie called *Chronique d'un été* (*Chronicle of a Summer*). I was holding a microphone and asking random passersby, "Are you happy?" Then I talked about you, the camps, your disappearance. It was a completely new way of making film, people told their stories and revealed who they were. The family reproached me for it. "Don't go and see that movie—Marceline shows off in it," one of my aunts ordered. Joris saw me in the film showing my tattooed number, talking about how you were gone but without ever looking sad, I think. But I didn't say I was happy. Joris knew the director and confided in him: "If I ever met that girl, I'd fall in love with her." And that's what happened. We were never apart from the moment we first met.

So he knew my story, and yours. We very rarely spoke about it, we didn't talk about ourselves very much at all. We behaved in a way so we'd never hurt each other. We thought of ourselves as a two-headed hydra; we traveled, made films together, dreamed of the future. In his memoirs, Joris wrote that we had the same desire: to rid the planet of its impurities. The word may be a bit too strong, but it's true, it fit with his idealism. We were living in the present, and we even thought we'd have some impact on history. That's a very strange feeling after you've been nothing but a *Stuck* in Birkenau.

But I'm talking to you about a time you never knew. Imagine the world after Auschwitz. When the wish to live replaces the wish to die. When rediscovered freedom spreads throughout the entire planet and demands new battles. Imagine Israel finally created! I thought about you so much, about how joyful you would have been. You

had always been a Zionist. Between the two wars,
you'd sent money to the Jewish National Fund
to buy back land in Palestine. You dreamed of a
future nation. You were investing, your brother
was already there. Would you have taken us there
if you'd survived? Would you have sold the château, your dream that had become a curse, and
chosen to leave? I would have gone with you. In
1947, a friend and I went to the office of a Jewish
organization that dealt with people who wanted to
go. I would have fought or helped there. They said
no, we were minors. There were already many survivors from the camps there, and I imagine they
didn't know what to do with them. We were young
girls, and damaged.

The world offered places to flee. While Israel
was being born, one after the other the people of
the countries colonized by the old European pow-
ers stood up for themselves and demanded their
independence. I was passionate about these political upheavals and the endless discussions they led
to. I thought, If I can't do anything for myself, I'm

going to do something for others. The Algerian uprising became the great cause of my generation, and for me, a test; I became an activist within the independence networks, lived outside the law, even watched the French police search my apartment, and I made a film about it, *Algérie, année zero* (*Algeria, Year Zero*), and it was banned for a long time. The more I demanded reparations for the Algerians, the more I felt I was being paid back myself, felt I'd found my place. They were Arabs and I was Jewish, but that wasn't the problem. I thought that by liberating other people, whether they were Algerian, Vietnamese, or Chinese, the Jewish problem would be solved at the same time. It was a terrible mistake, as the future proved, but I firmly believed it then.

And yet, years before, after we'd first been arrested, in my cell at Sainte-Anne, the holding place before Drancy and Birkenau, I'd said that I didn't trust people. I was nearly sixteen and a self-declared Gaullist. One of my fellow prisoners was a Resistance fighter and a Communist, and

she asked me why I wasn't. "I don't like the working classes," I'd replied, "because they're the ones
who carry out the pogroms." I spoke as a Jewish
woman, without even knowing where I was being
taken. I probably thought a little like you. I didn't
understand much of the discussions I'd overheard
at home between you and your brother Herman,
a proud Communist who'd gone to fight with
the International Brigades in Spain, or with Bill,
Mama's brother, who also went to fight Franco,
but I could sense what was at stake—saving the
world, saving ourselves, the Jews—and I understood that they reproached you for being a mod-
erate. We'd all listened intently to Radio London,
where they broadcast that Jews were being gassed
in trucks. You should know that Bill died a hero:
He killed the German Gestapo officer who was
interrogating him, then threw himself out of the
fourth-floor window.

Fifteen years later, it was my turn to ask myself
about the future of man. I hadn't become an opti-
mist. I would shiver in the waiting room of a train

station. In hotels, I refused to go into any bath-
room that had a shower. I couldn't stand the sight
of factory chimneys. When you've come back,
you're aware of such things as long as you live.
But in order to live, the best thing I could find to
believe in, to the point of obsession, like my uncles
before me, was that it was possible to change the
world.

Joris and I filmed the war in Vietnam; there
I earned the respect of the fighters for having
survived the death camps. And we wanted to
believe in the Chinese Revolution. I don't know
what the papers you read before the war said
about China, it was so far away, but at that time
Joris was already there making a movie; he had
filmed the peasants fighting the Japanese inva-
sion and still had contacts there. In fact, when
the Communists took control of the country, he
was on their side, hoping that this time the ideal
wouldn't turn out to be the totalitarian night-
mare it became in the USSR. He took me there.
We made about fifteen movies that were very

well received throughout the world. In France, we were taken as propagandists for the great Communist devil and its millions of ants in blue uniforms. We wanted to build a bridge between the East and the West, we wanted to study the society that claimed to change the relationship between men, we tried to listen to the Chinese people rather than their leaders, whose censorship and excesses we understood only too well. We were seeking the idea of revolution itself, in vain. Our movies opened with Chinese tales, where people were trying to move mountains.

I was probably a woman under the influence. I was obsessed with Joris. But I needed that dependency, the strength and convictions of a man like him. He was the school I'd never finished. The love that would save me. He represented a land far away. The antidote to your absence. I often disagreed with him, and told him so. I liked the idea of revolution, but I wasn't a Communist; I'd spent time with the Party for a few months but rejected it rather than back the

Soviet reign of terror. I sowed a seed of doubt in Joris's mind. He wrote about it in his memoirs. *"How could two people who were so close to one another in their aspirations, their revolt, their sense of justice, find themselves so far removed on ideological questions? It was the moment when I had to take a position and try to see what was fair and what wasn't."* I like those lines—they express how we complemented one another, they show our mistakes and how we tried to find our way, as well as how sincere we were.

It's futile trying to describe things to a dead man: years, countries, people, films he'll never know. And yet, I caught myself, just the other day, talking to you out loud about China. Just like that, alone in my Paris apartment, I was telling you that certain major universities in China have started courses on Judaism and the Talmud. I was forging links and similarities between the Chinese and our people. Between the Chinese people and me. I remembered that even when I was very little, China played a part in my dreams. That in school, we were told to sell the silver wrappers from chocolate bars to send money to the Chinese children who were victims of the famine; and after the war, I liked opening the door to a bookstore in the 5th arrondissement that was full of books with bone clasps; and the first time I went to China and ate wontons, I thought of the kreplach we had at home. I talked to you as if to vindicate myself. I was really only talking to myself. A long time ago, in the middle of my life without you, I cloaked myself in illusions, became frozen on the inside so I wouldn't have to think about anything anymore, so I could run away. And so I distanced myself from you.

Joris died in 1989, when China was experiencing the student uprising he'd so hoped for. "What's happening in China?" he asked from his deathbed. We held our breath with the rest of the world. He died along with the bloody crushing of the rebellion. Victim of a dream that had gone so wrong. The Italian newspaper *la Repubblica* wrote: "The final crime of Deng Xiaoping was the death of Joris Ivens." His death devastated me.

Henri said: "You ended up marrying your father." He said "your father," not "our father." I was shocked at the time. Then I thought about it. He hadn't taken your place—that was impossible; he hadn't been a protector—I'd taken care of him as much as he'd taken care of me. We were two artists, two recluses. But I had married a man of your age, an heir to the exalted nineteenth century that believed in the continuous, automatic progression of History. I had loved a man you would have loved. Joris had surely understood that as well, but he never spoke to me about it. And he too left me alone in the ruins of the twentieth century.

His friend, the photographer Henri Cartier-Bresson, opened a roll of film and wrote a message on it for him. He entrusted me with it, saying: "Do whatever you want with this." I didn't read it, I decided it was for Joris. I put it in his pocket so he would be less alone. And from me, a little globe of the world, the world we had traveled and dreamed about together. Then I let them close his coffin.

Afterwards, without really having made a conscious decision, I returned to you. It happened during a film festival in Warsaw, in 1991. I'd been invited to go and introduce the last film Joris and I had made together. It's called *Une histoire de vent* (*A Tale of the Wind*), we'd made it knowing there wouldn't be another. In it, Joris tries to find the wind, and his breath as well; the story says that when the earth breathes, that's what's called "the wind." At first, I refused the invitation—I didn't want to set foot in Poland again. They insisted so much that I finally said yes, but on condition that I could go to Auschwitz-Birkenau.

That was when I discovered something: We'd been so close to one another. I walked on your side, among the barracks and dormitories of Auschwitz. I'd never gone there, I didn't know which block you were in, I had no reference point. Then I looked for the place where you'd slipped me the onion and the tomato. It was on a road, but which one? I never found it. Then I concentrated on Birkenau. I remembered it in great detail. I saw a fox sleeping in the ruins of the crematorium. People who lived nearby went through on bicycles, the way you take a shortcut. I picked up a music stand the camp orchestra had used, and a spoon, so precious in the past—they were both rusted and half-buried in the ground. The place was empty. Then everything came back to me in a rush: the smell, the cries, the dogs, Françoise, Mala, the sky, red and black because of the flames. Then I found my bed and lay down on it.

Ten years later, I made a movie about that moment.* I wanted to walk through the mirror, clear a pathway, touch the imagination of everyone who hadn't been there. I'm not sure I succeeded. How can we hand down something we have so much difficulty in explaining to ourselves? I asked the actress Anouk Aimée to take my place, to stretch out on the prison bed and speak the words I'd said to you: "I loved you so much that I was happy to have been deported with you."

---

* *La petite prairie aux bouleaux* (*The Birch-Tree Meadow*), 2003 (Trans.)

I'm eighty-six years old, twice the age you were when you died. I'm an elderly lady now. I'm not afraid to die, I don't panic. I don't believe in God, or that there's anything after death. I'm one of the 160 still alive out of the 2,500 who came back—76,500 French Jews were sent to Auschwitz-Birkenau. Six million Jews died: in the camps, killed and thrown into mass graves, gassed, shot at point-blank range, massacred in the ghettos. Once a month, I have dinner with some friends who survived, we laugh together, even about the camp, in our own way. And I see Simone too. I've watched her take teaspoons in cafés and restaurants and slip them into her handbag; she'd been a minister, an important woman in France, an imposing person, but she still hoards worthless teaspoons so she doesn't have to lap up the terrible soup of Birkenau. If you only knew, all of you, how the camp remains permanently within us. It remains in all our minds, and will until we die.

Today, I have a lump in my throat. I often lose my temper. I don't know how to detach myself from the outside world—it kidnapped me when I was fifteen. The world is a hideous medley of communities and religions pushed to the extreme. And the hotter things get, the more unclear and important everything becomes, the more it has to do with us, the Jews. I now know that anti-Semitism is an eternal given; it rushes in waves along with the crises in the world, the words, the monsters, and the means of every era. Zionists like you predicted it: Anti-Semitism will never disappear. It is too deeply rooted in the world.

When the century stumbled into 2000, then 2001, something terrible happened, something unthinkable to me, impossible to describe to you who had left this world so long before: Two planes flown by terrorists crashed into the two highest skyscrapers in New York, the whole world saw it on television, the towers disintegrated, I watched people throw themselves out of the windows to escape the fires, and I was completely torn up inside. But everything became clear as well, the illusions I still had fell from me like dead skin. I don't know if that horror reawakened the other horror, but from that day on, I felt how much it meant to me to be a Jew. It was as if, up until that day, I'd been avoiding the fact that being Jewish is the strongest thing about me.

I feel like I'm the disillusioned heir of your illusions, an extension of you, the child born of your escape. You dreamed of America; well, the first time I went to New York, the city drew me in, I never wanted to leave, and I realized I was pursuing your exile. You dreamed of Israel, it exists. I feel good every time I go there, but it isn't the land of peace we'd hoped for. Israel has been at war ever since it was created. Wars normally end, but not this one, for the Jewish state has never been accepted by the Arab countries that surround it; its borders are never fixed, ever-changing, violent. And the longer this goes on, the more suspect Israel becomes, in the opinion of Europeans as well. I can hear a response in my mind, a film called *Welcome in Vienna.** It retraces our history, the history of European Jews. One of the characters says: "They will never forgive us for the evil they've done us." I've always been in favor of the coexistence of Israel and a Palestinian state, but I've become more and more moved by what is happening and what I'm hearing. I don't want to judge, I don't live there, but I will never have a single doubt when it comes to the right of Israel to exist. I will follow your dream.

You had chosen France, she isn't the melting pot you'd hoped for. Everything is getting tense again. We're called "French Jews"; there are also French Muslims, and here we are, face-to-face—I who had hoped never to take sides, or at least, to simply be on the side of freedom. I've listened to threats that sounded like echoes from the past, I've heard people shouting "Death to the Jews" and "Jews, fuck off, you don't own France," and I've wanted to throw myself out the window. Day

---

* The final movie, made in 1986, in a trilogy by Axel Corti (Trans.)

by day, I'm losing my convictions, the nuances, some of my memories; I end up questioning my past commitments; I see policemen outside of synagogues but I do not want to be someone who needs protection.

I lived because you wanted me to live. But I've lived the way I learned to back there, taking one day at a time. And there were some beautiful days, in spite of everything. Writing to you has helped me. When I talk to you, I don't feel consoled. But I release what is clasped tightly in my heart. I would like to run away from the history of the world, from this century, go back to my own time, the time of Shloïme and his darling little girl. That way I can return to my childhood, to the adolescence that was stolen from me, and that's normal at my age.

Two years ago, I asked Henri's wife, Marie: "Now that we are approaching the end of our lives, do you think it was a good thing for us to have come back from the camps?" "No, I don't," she replied, "we shouldn't have come back. But what do you think?" I couldn't say whether she was right or wrong; all I said was: "I'm starting to think like you." But I hope that if someone asks me that question just before I'm about to die, I'll be able to say, "Yes, it was worth it."